THE WORK OF THE MINISTRY

THE
WORK OF THE
MINISTRY

How to fulfil the Vision and Purpose
God has for Your Life

Boni Daniel

I dedicate this book to men with God's vision, people in ministry and believers interested in advancing Christ's kingdom.

God is able to make all grace abound toward you; that ye, always having all sufficiency in all things may abound to every good work. For He is able to do exceeding abundantly above all that we ask or think according to the power that worketh in us.

He that ministereth seed to the sower both ministered bread for your food, and multiply your seed sown, and increase the fruits of your righteousness, unto Him be glory in your work, ministry and activities by Christ Jesus throughout all generations, forever and ever! Amen. (2 Corinthians 9:8, 10; Ephesians 3:20)

When it comes to kingdom work it involves winning souls, making disciples and the gift of ministry which involves improving the quality of life in the world. That is why doing God's kingdom work not only is winning souls and making disciples but also by improving the quality of life in our communities.

Believers are to function as heaven on earth. We are sent into the world as salt and light. We should understand the breadth of the mission of Christ to bring God's kingdom and will on earth as it is in heaven. (Luke 11:2-4)

We all have our unique gifts and calling and we are made in the image of God to do great works like Jesus.

Through faith in God and His word, we can believe God for the miraculous. Reading the word with the help of the spirit, we can receive faith to access God's promises. There is miraculous and transforming power in the scripture. Searching the scriptures can bring inner transformation and personal closeness to Christ. Long lasting blessing is tied to personal transformation through humility and dependence on God to empower us in His own abilities. God empowers man with natural abilities to help reduce human suffering on the earth. It is given by God and I pray for the exceeding grace of God in you.

Thanks be unto God for His unspeakable gift. (2 Corinthians 9:15)

Table Of Contents

God wants to use you to impact your world for Jesus Christ. He will create circumstances in order for you to respond to His call. He will even prosper you materially to do it and to encourage you to this end. The Spirit of the Lord is here to move you into a God plan for your good. He will help you to achieve the purposes for which He made you. The word of God gives us a glimpse of an example of heaven's purpose in man's life. The Lord said to Jeremiah, "Before I formed thee in the belly I knew thee; and before thou comest forth out of the womb I sanctified thee, and I ordained thee a prophet unto the nations. (Jeremiah 1:5)

The Holy Spirit is here on the earth, conferring with the Lord about the plan and purpose of God for your life. Will you agree with God's plan for your life to achieve the purposes for which God made you?

This is the very thing God does in many who have been called for a special mission. The prophets, the apostle and many men receive a personal visitation from Jesus, through the Holy Ghost. There are many example of God bringing divine visitation in the lives of those He called for His purpose.

We can embrace that calling if we are open to the Holy Spirit's work in us. We can actually thank God for His visit that was required to get us to this purpose. Would you be willing to sit with the Lord for your life and agree with the plans God has for your life? Could you give God complete freedom to implement that plan no matter the cost? Ask God to give you the grace and trust in His love for you.

Also, the Holy Spirit is here to help you to better understand the work that is important. It gives us an outlet for our skills and talents. The work we do in His kingdom is an expression of who we are which means that if you are a Christian, your work is an expression of your understanding of who you are in Christ. The word of God has to teach us about what we should be doing, and how we should be doing it. Along the way, His spirit is here to teach us what God is calling us to do with our life.

The blessings of God make us rich with goods and possessions so that we will sponsor kingdom work here on the earth. We are stewards of His wealth or riches and what we have belongs to God and for His service, to refuse to give Him or give for His work means robbing God of His treasure or possession. The blessings of God are for the work of God not for our pleasure or self–satisfaction. God does not want you to die premature. He wants you to live to fulfill your purpose and to advance His kingdom on earth. (Psalm 91:1-16; Psalm 128:1-2, Psalm 92:13-15, Psalm 145:19-20)

Doing His kingdom work here on the earth simply means bringing righteousness, peace and joy in the Holy Ghost into the hearts and lives of men. God wants you to live to bring joy, peace and hope into the lives of the people. God wants to comfort His people through you. God is in the business of bringing life, form and order into the lives of His creatures through His Spirit. When the earth was without form, void and darkness was upon the face of the waters, God moved by His spirit and bring beauty, light and good things into the earth. (Genesis 1:2) Without God, this world would be a total mess and it would not be good or conducive to live. Also without Him, men on the earth would not be good. If God took away all the good men of this world, this world would become bad and evil and wickedness would be everywhere. That is why God wants you to live long, to fulfill His will and purpose in your life. In other words, God wants you to live and do God things, and bring joy and blessings to the people.

In essence, we must do the work of Him that sent us. We should advance and does His kingdom work here on earth. Jesus says, "…for the works which the Father hath given me to finish, the same works that I do, bear witness of me, that the Father hath sent me." (John 5:36 b)

Beloved, I wish above all things that God; the author of all knowledge, wisdom and all good work will inspire you in every good work. The anointing is God's wisdom for men's dominion on the earth. It is like the oil of the spirit that helps us keep moving and enables us to do kingdom work. God, who knows everything from the beginning to the end, is the one in the right position to lead or guide you in life and when you have faith in God, He has all the insight to provide for your needs. He will arrange all that it takes for you to have or receive all that it takes to do it.

His intent is to help us develop Christ likeness so that we become salt and light in the world. (Matthew 5:13-14) As the facets of His character are infinite, so the ways God provides for us are beyond anything we can ask or imagine. (Ephesians 3:20) We can trust His goodness, guidance and shepherding care to do more for us than we could ever achieve on our own.

A call to His work is a call to the love of God. He has given us gifts differing according to the grace that is given to us, weather prophecy, ministry, teaching, exhortation, giving, etc. This love of God is without dissimulation. It abhors that which is evil, cleaves to that which is good, it is kindly affection to human need and to the necessity of mankind. Not slothful in business and fervent in spirit serving the Lord. This love of God makes you to be creative, to ease the pain of others, or to solve the problems of others. Jesus says by this love the world will know that we are His disciples.

This love of Christ that comes to us from a sanctified heart opens to us the door of God sufficiently. Your sufficiency is from God. God knows how to bless you when He wants to bless you. Don't dictate to Him the way to bless you. Live everything to Him, to do things His way or the way He chooses to do it. God is able to finance His work or project on the earth through His ways.

Also, a call to His work is a call to function as heaven on earth. We are sent into the world as salt and light. We all have our unique gifts and calling and we are made in the image of God to do great works like Jesus.

I will conclude with the words of the Psalmist who says, "How precious also are thy thoughts unto me, O God! How great is the sum of them!" (Psalm 139:17) And to add it good, "I will praise thee; for I am fearfully and wonderfully made: marvelous are thy works; and that my soul knoweth right well." (Psalm 139:14)

May He satisfy us with His mercy that we may rejoice and be glad all our days and let His work appear unto His servants, and His glory unto their children. And let the beauty of the LORD our God be upon us: and establish thou the work of our hands upon us; yea, the work of our hands establish thou it. (Psalm 90:14; 90:16-17)

Chapter One

The Road To The Ministry Or Work Of God

Ministry simply means duty or service to humanity or service for the course of God. It is an act or the process of helping or caring.

God is still working on the earth. He is the sustainer of all things that He created and without His grace and mercy human suffering would become unbearable. God is involved in sustaining His cosmic world. In science, we assume that the laws of the universe are regular and will continue to function. This is only an assumption as there is no reason for it unless God keeps it this way. God is the cosmic law giver and sustainer.

…And upholds all things by the word of His power… (Hebrew 1:3, see also Colossian 1:17)

Dreams and vision for something comes from God. (Acts 1:17-21) God gives man dreams and vision to create, to make or start something good.

He created man in His image and gives man the power of creativity, technology and innovation. Man is God's masterpiece, designed to do good works. God is master brain and designer of the cosmic (the universe seen as an ordered system). Praise for human genius must first begin with acknowledging or given glory to God, the only real creator. We should know better now that most human individual genius was only possible because man was made in the image and likeness of this creator of the universe (Genesis 1:26), who alone gave man the capability to be self-aware, to think, create, dream and design products or things that have revolutionized the earth realm.

It is God that gives man vision for innovation and enterprise or investments that will improve life for human beings. Vision and dreams are solutions to the problems of mankind.

Do Not Despise the Days of Little Beginning

The Bible encourages us not to despise our little beginning. I love the fire, that certain drive inside, which propels people to seek to make a difference in this generation of people and touch their lives.

When Bill and Paul Allen started Microsoft, their vision of a computer on every desktop and in every home seemed farfetched to most people.

Today, that vision is a reality in many parts of the world and personal technology is an integral part of society.

You are called for a righteous purpose. God uses whoever He wills and whatever He wills. God has called us in righteousness that is for a righteous purpose to spread His Gospel. Will you be available for God's use today?

God's Act, Power or Miracle is involved in the Coming and Formation of Ministry

Unaided intellect cannot know truth. I am glad that the spirit is the giver of the force that creates, if things were up to me, I would have messed it up and lost it a long time ago. Our success and achievement belong to him: he started it; he maintains it and he will finish it for his glory. You cannot mess it up! You have a God given vision, you are heaven connected. Just stay in his will.

For any meaningful ministry to take place, God's power must act to enable, protect and preserve that which is to be born or come into the world.

Revelation of the word brings into existence that which never existed before. Also, God's power preserves what He wants to do in our life. When Boko haram overwhelmed my home town, Mubi,

Adamawa State in Nigeria, destroying lives, buildings and properties, the Lord saved my life through a safe exit. When I was in Abuja, during the period of the Boko haram stay in Mubi, the Lord gave me a revelation that God will preserve His writings. When I returned home after the Boko haram insurgent were killed and wiped out from Mubi, I discovered that some of the Boko haram members lived inside our houses and used some of our things. But to the glory of God, they did not enter my room and all my written articles and many book manuscripts were safe and secure.

When God gives you a revelation, you can be sure that no devil can stop you from having it or getting your expectation and heart's desire. One of the functions of the Holy Spirit in our lives is to confirm to us what God will do in our lives. He will also confirm to you the miracles of God that has taken place in your life or the miracle that will take place in your life.

When you receive your victory in the spirit, rest assured that God will give you victory. What controls the external (physical) is the spiritual. It has already been concluded in the spirit world. The Holy Spirit ministers to our human spirit and when He speaks there will be peace and assurance in the heart.

The Route to the Work

When you are filled with the spirit, you will have the anointing. Anointing is God's grace and ability to do something good.

The anointing is the route to the work of God and also the work of innovation and creation of something good for the need of man.

Anointing is like a certificate of recognition from God to accomplish a given task or purpose. It is a mark of service to God and humanity.

Anointing is a divine enablement that makes you to do or accomplish something in life. Anointing can be said to be a gift or talent from God that enables you to do something.

Joyce Meyer writes, "We really must walk in love because that aids and increases the anointing on our lives and the anointing is what enable us to do what God has called us to do. Again, God's anointing is presence and power and that enables us to do with ease what could never be accomplished with any amount of struggle on our own. We all need God's anointing. A person does not have to work at a so called "spiritual" job to need God's anointing. We need it to parent, to survive in the world, to be good friends, on the job, and literally in everything we do."[1]

Also, anointing is the route to God service or call of God for our lives. God does not want you to go to the ministry or mission field without the anointing. Anointing enables you to stand on the word of God and get results.

In Luke 4:14, "Jesus returned in the power of the Spirit into Galilee; and there went out a fame of him throughout the entire region round about."

Anointing creates influence; it enables you make an impact to your generation. It launches you to the open.

The Call to His Work

In John 5:17 Jesus says, "My father is always at his work to this very day, and I too am working." (NIV)

The Psalmist declared, "When I consider the heavens, the work of thy fingers, the moon and the stars, which thou hast ordained; what is man that thou art mindful of him? And the son of man, that thou visitest him? The heavens declare the glory of God; and the firmament showeth his handy work.

---

[1]Joyce Meyer, the power of simple prayer (New York: faith words, Hachette Book Group, USA), P 221.)

Day unto day uttered speech, and night unto night showed knowledge. There is no speech nor language, where their voice is not heard. (Psalm 19:1-3)

It is God that reveals knowledge, things and work for man to do. "I will praise thee; for I am fearful and wonderfully made; marvelous are thy works; and that my soul knoweth right well." (Psalm 139:14)

In John 6:27-29 Jesus said, "Labour not for the meat which perisheth, but for that meant which endureth unto everlasting life, which the son of man shall give unto you; for him hath God the father seated." Then said they unto him, "What shall we do, that we might work for the good." (Romans 8:28) We do God's work by the grace God has given (you) us. We are all building on the work God started. We are building on it. Each one should build on the area of ministry God called him to do. We are God's temple and that God's spirit lives among us (you) and works through us and it will be rewarded, the worker will receive a reward from Him.

Therefore, my dear brothers and sisters, stand firm. Let nothing move you. Always give yourselves fully to the work of the Lord because you know that your labour in the Lord is not in vain. (1 Cor. 15:58)

It is the spirit who is now at work in us, that is, it is the spirit who is now doing the work of God in us. The spirit is now at work in those who are obedient to the ruler of the kingdom of God. For we are God's handy-work, created in Christ Jesus to do good works, which God prepared in advance for us to do. (Ephesians 2:10)

And the word of God gives us this confident, that He who began a good work in you will carry it on to completion until the day of Christ Jesus. (Philippians 1:6)

As we are doing the things He commands us, He is here to deliver. He will strengthen us and protect us from the evil one. He is also here to direct your hearts into God's love and equip you for every good work.

chapter two

The Need For God's Power To Change The World

The work of God is commissioned on the earth through power, and this power enables men to minister to the needs of the people. The power of God is displayed for effective evangelism that is in any effective evangelism we see the power of God displayed power from on high enables signs, wonders and miracles in life and ministry work.

The scriptures are replete with passages equating the knowledge of God with His display of the supernatural e.g. Abraham and Sarah having a child past the normal biological age, Moses doing signs and wonders in Egypt, so that His power may be demonstrated to the world (Romans 9:17), or Elijah calling down fire from heaven to demonstrate that the Lord is the true God (1 Kings 18). These and many more scriptures in the Old Testament are replete with examples like these.

What about the New Testament? First of all, Jesus told His disciples that they would receive power to be His witnesses. (Acts 1:8) This power was primarily cantered on the ability to be a witness of the resurrection Christ. The Biblical narratives after Acts 1:8 shows that the primary reason for this power was that the apostles would demonstrate the words by healing the sick and performing miracles. Acts 5:12-16 connected extraordinary signs and wonders with God adding multitudes of believers to the Lord.

The disciples of Jesus turn the whole city to the Lord by moving in the power of signs, wonders and miracles. Acts 14:3 says that the Lord bore witness to the word of His grace by granting signs and wonders to be done by the hands of Paul while he was ministering in the city of Ephesus. Later on, as recorded in Acts 23:1-10, Paul was able to bring the gospel to the whole island of Malta after he healed the chief man of the Island whose name was Pablius. Also, God supernaturally spared Paul's life after a poisonous snake, which was supposed to kill him, bit him. There was always a demonstration of the Holy Spirit and power when Paul preached the word so that people's faith would not rest on the wisdom of man but on the power of God. (1 Corinthians 2:1-4)

The supernatural move of the Holy Spirit was a normal occurrence in the lives of all the early churches as we read in Paul's letter to the Galatians in verse 3:5. God supplied their church with the Spirit and miracles through the hearing of faith.

Furthermore, Hebrews 6:5 says that believers during those days experienced the power of the age to come. If we take the context of this book and the whole New Testament, this passage is referring to the power of the invisible, supernatural God, intervening in the lives of men through miraculous healing, supernatural signs and wonders.

Hebrews 2:4 also says that the Lord bore witness to the word from the Lord Jesus and His apostle by granting them signs, wonders and various miracles and gifts of the Holy Spirit. If the apostles of the first country needed to depend upon God's power to preach the gospel, perform signs and wonders, how much more should we depend upon this to do the work of the ministry, to bring the present generation of the reality of Jesus?

If Jesus Christ our Lord and Saviours needed the power, how much more does the present day believers need to depend upon the power of God to do the work of the ministry and to change the world for good?

Commission with Power

The kingdom of God here on the earth is commission through His power or force. Faith invites the presence and power of God to come and do the will, purpose and word of God in our heart or to do the will and vision of God in our lives. Faith invites the presence and power of God into our lives, to come and do that which God ordained or says concerning us, His plan for your life.

When we are born of the Spirit, we conceived the physical life of the son of God and you and I conceive the vision of God when we are born again. From that moment on, we are essentially two people on the inside. We have the mind, emotions, and will that we were physically born with but we now also have the mind, emotions and will of Christ with us. We have a spiritual implant of the life of Jesus Christ within our bodies.

This is actually Jesus in the person of the Holy Spirit. This implanting of the life of Christ is a supernatural miracle. It is something God does in response to our humble and deliberate personal faith in His word.

God's greatness has not been diluted in any way over the years of time. He is just as great today as he has been in the past. He can lead our entire life so that we can find peace and fulfilment. He is able to lead us in the right direction that will be pleasing to Him and good for us.

The Holy Spirit leads men to the accurate wisdom of the truth. What did the Lord Jesus Christ tell us? He said, "I have yet many things to say unto you, but you cannot bear them now. Howbeit when He, the Spirit of Truth is come, He will guide you into all truth." (John 16:12-13) Therefore, there is no wise man in the world; we are all drawing light from above. The issue before us is about simple learning from the spirit of truth. The scriptures have advised that whosoever thinks himself wise, let him be a fool that he may be wise, because the wisdom of this world is foolishness before God.

The Bible indicates that the Holy Spirit is a spirit of great understanding and knowledge. (Isaiah 11:2) He will teach us things that we never learned down here. Sir Isaac Newton stated, when an old man said to one who praised his wisdom, "I am as a child on the sea shore picking up a pebble here and a shell there, but the great ocean of faith still lies before me." Thomas Edison once said, "I do not know one million part of one percent about anything, our loving father, His Spirit will give us great understanding and knowledge of things that we never know."

He reveals profound mysteries beyond man's understanding. He knows all hidden things, for he is light... (Daniel 2:22 TLB)

The Spirit of God is the force of creation. Psalm 104:30 corroborated this: "Thou you send your spirit and new life is born to replenish all the living of the earth." (TLB) There will be a creation when the Spirit of God moved. (Genesis 1:1-2)

Creation still takes place today. The Spirit of God has not stopped moving and causing people to create things, and creation is still taking place and progressing. When the Spirit of God begins to move, changes will take place in a man's life, situations and circumstances. When the Spirit of God moves in your life, things will change for you, from zero to glory, from failure to success, from sickness to healing and good health.

Everything that needs recreation in your life shall be recreated by the Spirit of God. Determine to receive His Spirit in your life. Pray for God's powerful spirit (Dunamis) to come upon your life. Pray for the spirit of revival. Pray O Lord, I welcome your Spirit into my life, let everything in me that needs life, recreation or beauty, be recreated, O Lord, in Jesus name.

When Dunamis power of God is at work in your life, it will cause all things (both the good and the bad) to work together for your own good and purpose.

Receive the Fire

Every visitation of God's purpose or innovation is preceded by fire. In Luke 1:35, the angel said to Mary, "The Holy Ghost shall come upon thee, and the power of the highest shall overshadow thee; therefore also that holy thing which shall be born of thee shall be called the son of God."

This message is coming to alert you of God's visitation upon your life. It is a great outpouring of the spirit of righteousness and power to do great exploits for God on the face of the earth. It is referring to the manifestation of God's presence and fire in your body. Every visitation of God brings something from God to His people; the people of God are not ready because we are in a most unready state. Unready to receive Christ, unready for His glory, unready for His power, unready for His blessings and unready for His return. You must be ready to receive from God.

The believers were unready. Why? Because they were not sanctified and their garments were filthy. Every child of God who wants to be part of the glory God is about to unleash unto the end time must be willing to be sanctified. To sanctify is to make separate and consecrate by the working power of the Holy Ghost and the word of God. You must submit yourself willingly for the Holy Ghost to clean you of every filthiness of your flesh and your Spirit. The Holy Ghost has a mandate from Jesus Christ to sanctify us unto Him. It is for our good and leaders must not shy away from their divine assignment. Every truth needs to be taught. The truth must not be handled in respect of persons.

If God is going to do wonders in our midst like He did of old, then we need to sanctify ourselves. If God will do wonders in your life and through your life then you need to separate, set apart unto God.

"And Joshua said unto the people, sanctify yourselves; for tomorrow the LORD will do wonders among you." (Joshua 3:5)

If you are seeking an encounter with God, prepare to receive His fire. If you are willing to be used by God, prepare to receive fire. If you wish to retain God's presence and glory for your generation, prepare yourself by His fire. The fire I speak of is spiritual not physical; a spiritual fire, for doing the right thing.

"But who may abide the day of His coming? And who shall stand when he appeared? For he is like a refiner's fire, and like fullers soap: and he shall sit as a refiner and purifier of silver: and he

shall purify the sons of Levi and purge them as gold and silver, that they may offer unto the LORD an offering in righteousness. " (Malachi 3:2-3)

The mystical creature, the phoenix, was referenced by early church leaders highlighting the beauty of reinvention with fire as both the impetus and the method for change. When we survive the refiner's fire we experience the transformation and saving nature of a God who is able to use all trials for His glory.

The fire of the Holy Ghost is behind the making of generational impact that cannot be erased. It is the Holy Ghost fire that imparts a life with the capacity to release potential. Through His Spirit you can receive the unique fire of God. He will place inside you the unique fire to fulfill your calling and purpose.

The Benefits Of The Anointing

The anointing is meant to give you a beautiful life here on earth and also prepare you for eternal reward in heaven. That is because there is a social aspect and a spiritual aspect of it. Also, there is a social implication of the anointing and there is spiritual implication of the anointing.

In Psalm 89:20-24 the Lord says, "I have found my servant David; with my holy oil I have anointed him, with whom my hand shall be strengthening him. The enemy shall not outwit him, nor the son of wickedness afflicts him. I will beat down his foes before his face and plaque those who hate him. But my faithfulness and my mercy shall be with him, and in my name his horn shall be exalted."

When God anoints you with His holy oil, He will steady you and make you strong. Your enemies shall not outwit you nor shall the wicked overpower you. He will beat down your adversaries before you. He will protect and bless you constantly and surround you with His love and you will be great because of God.

The anointing is the supernatural force to have dominion over everything that God made (including the devil). The anointing is God's wisdom for man's dominion on the earth (Genesis 1:26), with it you can be able to quench all the fierce darts of the devil. (Ephesians 6:16)

The anointing also teaches man about all things. (1 John 2:27) That is the anointing is like a teacher and lives within you, in your hearts, so that to teach you what is right. The anointing is truth and no liar, so just as the anointing teaches you all things, you must live in Christ, never to depart from Him.

No matter what it teaches, you must learn to stand on the truth. The truth sets free, Jesus said, "And ye shall know the truth, and the truth shall make you free." (John 8:32)

Truth is differed from the facts of life. In this world we have facts based on natural laws.

Facts are information that are restricted to human realm or lesser realm. As far as Jesus is concerned, any information you gain can be false. Your success comes better when you listen to Jesus. You need to have the word of God. Jesus is the truth that is what He says is the finality (final), and what heaven says concerning your case that is the final.

How Can You Know You Are Standing on Truth

The truth of God is the voice of God to you at a time. When you hear the voice of God, no human being can handle you on earth or put you into bondage.

The truth is revealed by the anointing or through the process of being studious in His word. Truth is revealed to you by God, or truth is by revelation of God to you.

Truth helps you to secure divine direction; it helps you to escape the bondage that is in this world and you become free.

Truth does not depend on facts. To apply it, you must know the truth of the matter before you act. When you discover the truth, which is the voice of God to you, you will be set free. The truth inspires faith in your life.

Facts demand that you call things the way they are but the truth is that God call the things that are not as though they were. (Romans 4:17) Abraham got that voice of God (truth) and stood on it. The truth of God is the voice of God to you. It destroys every iota of doubt.

If you want it, read Habakkuk 2:1. Stand upon your watch, and set yourself upon the tower, and watch to see what He will say to you.

Also, another benefit of the anointing is oil for the work. A Christian that does not have the spirit is a struggling Christian and he will do little exploit and not be able to achieve a lot for God.

The Spirit translates the word of God and makes it into something new. You are reading not only the letter word of God but a life giving spirit of God, resting on the word. (See John 6:63)

The anointing is the way to break a strong heart to obedience and also give a door for God to effectively use you. (Romans 15:18-21) Treasure in an earthen vessel is the anointing. (2 Corinthians 4:7)

Summary

Anointing is meant to give you a beautiful life on earth because one of the benefits of anointing is to make you great. (Psalm 89:20-24)

When you are consistent on a particular thing the anointing stays. The anointing comes as God finds you doing something. How do we get the anointing? The answer is by doing something. When God finds you doing it, He pours out the anointing. Especially when doing good.

Do something consistently and a time will come when God will lay His hands on you or on it.

Also, there are different areas of the anointing e.g. Daniel's life shows anointing for holiness and David was great in battle. The anointing in the life of Abraham is to believe God for faith.

The seven (7) spirits of God are also areas of anointing.

chapter four

Real Perspective On Ministry And Kingdom Work

Ministry work centers on using your gift to help believers or people. It relents with the vision and purpose of God for your life. Ministry work centre on using your spiritual gift for the edification and building of believers and also improving the quality and life of humanity. When it comes to ministry, as each one has received a gift, he should be faithfully administering God's grace to people.

While kingdom work centres on doing God's work, it relents to doing and advancing the course of Christ or God.

Ministry centres on giving while kingdom work centres on reaching. Kingdom work is for reaching people to save their souls. That is reaching people with the word of God or salvation message of God.

Kingdom work deals with drawing people to God while ministry centres on giving to the people.

While kingdom work centres on reaching or drawing people to God through Christ, ministry work centres on giving to the people or believers and also giving to the community. For example, we have men with the gift of giving. And in giving, when you give God replenishes you. He waters you and provides you with more or many doors of blessing; financially prosperity or receiving. When you release to nature, nature releases it back to you and when you give out, it gives you back more in return.

The Kingdom of God

The kingdom of God here on the earth is righteousness, peace and joy in the Holy Ghost. The Bible says that God is love. Everything God does is impelled and influenced by His love. (1 John 4:7-8) God's love is agape and it refers to a benevolent, charitable love that seeks the best for the loved one. It involves the caring provision of God, our deep friendship with Him, His passionate love and fatherhood for His children, the fatherly love of God to us, and His love is selfless. The Bible says that God was motivated by love to save the world. (John 3:16) God's love is best seen in the sacrifice of

Jesus on our behalves. His love is gracious. (1 John 4:9)

God demonstrates His own love for us, while we were still sinners, Jesus died for us. (Romans 5:8) He is the initiator of a loving relationship with us. Any love we have for God is simply a response to His sacrificial love for us. He loves us and sent His son as an atoning sacrifice for our sins. (1 John 4:10)

God's love for us in Christ Jesus has resulted in our being brought into His family. (1 John 3:1) Our heavenly Father receives us with joy when we come to Him in faith. He makes us accepted in the beloved. (Ephesians 1:6)

The Bible says that we are to love others the way Jesus loves us. We are to preach and make disciples of all the nations. (Matthew 28:19) The Bible says that our love for God is related to our obedience of Him. (1 John 5:3, John 14:15) God's desire is that the world might be saved through Jesus Christ. (John 3:17)

God's love for sinners is why Jesus died on the Cross. May we use the greatest work that He has done in our lives – His love gift (His salvation) to pave the way for mankind to experience His free gift of eternal life. May God help us to respond to His love by loving our fellow brethren and those that are unbelievers, may He help us to be humble and loving. We pray this not with our might nor by power but by His Spirit in Jesus Christ. May we be a crown of splendor in the Lord's hands (Isaiah 62:3)

How to Run with Kingdom Work

Kingdom work is always done in partnership with God. You cannot do the work of God without God, and you cannot do it without partnership with God because God is the one doing the work through a human vessel or medium. No matter what God may lead or direct you to do, the end will always be that He is the one who will do the invisible work in the heart of His people or children. For example, it is God Himself who will convince them, put thoughts in their hearts and mind, speak to them in a vision or dream and direct them to supply the need at ground or kingdom or ministry needs and provision.

So, God will be the end result of the work of the kingdom or ministry. You may appeal or ask for what a ministry needs but only God has the power to convince and direct the people through His Spirit so that they will be able to give. That is why Jesus Says, "A man can receive nothing until it is given to him from above." God is the giver of all things, without Him you cannot receive anything, even the people that comes to you is not by your own ability but it is God that allows the people to come your way or come to you. So, we can only receive what God gives or appoints unto us. It is the grace of God that enables you to have what you get.

It is God that will do the invisible for you. Because the work of God can only be done in partnership with God. The only way to have the hands of God move in your life or ministry is through resorting to prayer. Prayer is very vital and important to a successful life and ministry. Prayer is vital and important to the ministry and also to the success of the ministry God has given to us. A minister must always be on the mount with God for the Spirit of God to move into the hearts of people, to convince people to repent, to put thoughts into their hearts, minds and emotions, to convince and direct them to give to God, to men and for the ministry, without Him we can do nothing on our own.

The Importance of People to the Kingdom or Ministry

People are very important to the work of God and to the ministry. It is good for ministers to know and understand the importance of the people in our lives and our ministry. God has a reason for bringing people our way and every group of people we have in our lives have their peculiar gifts, talents and advantage.

Some people can be very important to us in our prayers. We need them to partner with us in prayers, we need them for prayers to the ministry, and others can be every important to us when it comes to partnership for the financial need of the ministry.

Some prayers of a God fearing and dedicated believer can be more important to you in your life and ministry more than the gift of any financial donor. Some people's mouth (utterance) or word can be a very powerful asset to us in our lives and ministry. Their prayers and consecrated lives can be very powerful to us. James said, "God chose the poor of this world to be rich in faith (James 2:5) and that the effective fervent prayers of a righteous man availed much." (James 5:16) Their fervent prayers can bring forth fruit in our lives and in our ministry.

Also for the people or believers who sow unto the things of God, God sees their heart and knows what they want. When we give, the scripture saith it will be given back to us. (Matthew 7:7-8)

Ministers themselves are the first givers; they give their lives, time, finances and resources for the work of God and God will bless them much in this life and in the life to come.

Ministry Work or Vision

Like kingdom work, ministry work is also done in response to a leading by the word of God or response of the Holy Spirit. Let the word of God and the Spirit of God lead and guide you on what you should do.

I discovered that there are many people who complain about giving to the ministry work or gospel work. This according to them is that ministers use the money on leisure and other materials things. My advice is that you let the word of God and the Spirit of God be your guide or lead. Let your life hope, dreams, etc. build on the word of God and the Spirit of God. Just do your part and let God do His part. God will Himself judge any minister who misuses His resources for personal gain or purposes. You are not in the position to judge God's ministers or anointed, let God do His work.

As you give, God will bless and reward you for your obedience to His word and leading of His Spirit. Jesus says, "Therefore, whosoever heareth His saying, and doeth them, He will liken him unto a wise man, which built his house upon a rock." (Matthew 2:27, Emphasis mine)

Your foundation should be God's word. "Heaven and earth shall pass away, but my words shall not pass away." (Mark 13:31) Unlike this world and everything in it, you can bank on the word. It will never change; the word is eternal. The word of God is the sure and firm foundation! Build your life on the word today and the leading of the Spirit today and not on human philosophies or human reason that changes with time. Jesus is the word of God made flesh (John 1:14) and His Spirit is here on earth. Let Him direct the course of your life today.

Ministry Work and the Financial Issues

God has many ways to finance His vision on earth. He can decide to finance it through a single person. I call it giant giver and also He can decide to finance it through individual givers that are His people giving in support of His work on the earth, and also He can decide to finance it through the minister himself (the recipient of the vision). I call it covenant giving that is God can decide to open doors for the minister through business and other financial sources and the minister will use the finances and resources to sponsor the vision, that is the minister will by himself sow into the vision of God for His life that is the God given vision and using what you have.

When the people of God refuse to heed or hear His word or leadings to help such a minister, through the minister or any individual God can raise a financial giant for His vision or purpose on the earth e.g. When the children of Israel refused to obey His word and commandments, God decided to raise a generation for Himself through Moses but Moses interceded for them.

The point here is that both the minister and His people should have a proper view or perspective about money or material things. At the end, whatever we acquire or accumulate for ourselves in this earth, we will not carry it after death. We will leave it here on the earth and also one day all the wealth of this earth will belong to the anti-Christ. So the best way to make wise use of our finances or investments is to use it for God's work and for the service of humanity.

At the end, only what we have done for God and mankind (humanity) will count up to eternity.

Partners for the Ministry

The work of the minister is to pray that God will Himself lay a burden in the heart of His people or children to sow into the ministry. As the word of God and the Spirit of God made a desire impact into their life, people will on themselves move to sow into the ministry.

The Spirit of God can put thoughts into people hearts that will make them respond to His leading or guidance because these are not just thoughts of a man but the word of God.

As a minister, your duty is to keep praying that God will communicate with His people to do things that will help you realize that vision. Ministers should bear in mind that is not oratory excellence or a neat pulpit that will make people give in support of the ministry but the secret is that by asking God to put a burden into the heart of His people to give in support of the ministry work. Only God can lead and direct people into His things.

Grace in Ministry Work

When it comes to the work of the gospel or ministry, work is given less consideration; God wants us to build on faith. Faith in His word and faith in His ability to provide all our needs.

We may not know how God operates or how His word will operate in our life but all we need to do is have faith in God and trust him that he will provide all our needs.

When God releases a vision, He makes provision. And His provision can come as a blessing in disguise. Joseph's prison became a way to receive his provision.

Also, the grace of God will preserve and protect you. The sovereign ruling of God is very wonderful. When Joseph was about to be killed by his brothers, God sent slave traders to buy him and take him to Egypt.

This is the same God that you serve; the God of Joseph is your God. When the enemy wants to get rid of you, God will send you help.

God want us to build on faith and His word. Galatians 2:16 says, "Knowing that a man is not justified by the works of the law, but by the faith of Jesus Christ, that we might be justified by the faith of Christ, and not by the works of the law; for by the works of the law shall no flesh be justified."

At the appointed time, what God has destined shall always prevail. Destiny can only be delayed but will never be denied.

How to Succeed in Your Life and Ministry

A successful life or ministry is faith based; don't depend on your work. You can simply pay the ministry bill through tithing and giving. When you are faithful to God in your giving, He will bless you and you will have the finances to pay your bills or sponsor the vision.

God said prove me in this giving and tithes and see if I will not open the gates of heaven and pour many blessings for you.

Through faith you can depend or rely on God to provide all your needs or finances. Riches do not come through hard work but you receive riches through God's favour.

Be not deceived; God is not mocked: for whatsoever a man soweth, that shall he also reap. For he that soweth to his flesh shall of the flesh reap corruption; but he that soweth to the Spirit shall of the Spirit reap life everlasting. And let us not be weary in well doing: for in due season we shall reap, if we faint not. As we have therefore opportunity, let us do good unto all men, especially unto them who are of the household of faith. (Galatians 6:7-10)

If the Lord makes room for you, you will be fruitful. The ways of the Lord is give or give it up, but the ways of the world is grasping or grasp it up.

The love of the world makes us spiritually blind; the way of the world makes us blind spiritually. Grasping and deceiving is the way or technique of the world. God does not need your help to make things happen. God wants you to obey His word. He wants you to be spiritual, to do it in a godly way. Are you building it in a godly way? To have your building or works in gold.

You will reap what you sow for no man fails in the grace of God. God's will is that all the families of the earth will be blessed through you. The primary purpose of filling in the spirit is that you will have the blessing of Abraham.

Galatians 3:13-14 says, "Christ hath redeemed us from the curse of the law, being made a curse for us: for it is written, Cursed is every one that hangeth on a tree: That the blessing of Abraham might come on the Gentiles through Jesus Christ; that we might receive the promise of the Spirit through faith."

God filled you with the spirit and gives you vision so that you will be a blessing to people.

chapter five

When God Commands

If you are dealing with God, you will learn to tune to His frequency. God gives man an authority to command. When you go to where He sends you, prophesy and He will sustain you by that prophecy.

When you are dealing with God, when He tells you something it will come to pass. Get God to tell you something. In 1 Kings 17:3-4, The Lord said to Elijah, "Get thee hence, and turn thee eastward, and hide thyself by the brook Kerith that is before Jordan. And it shall be, that thou shalt drink of the brook; and I have commanded the ravens to feed thee there." Elijah did not negotiate with the raven to feed him, he dealt with God and God sustained him through the raven.

Man is like grass, he is today but tomorrow he is no more, man can fail you but not God. His word never fails.

It is God that gives or provides so don't negotiate with man because man can fail you. Go to God and negotiate it with Him through prayer and God will surely make it to come to you or become yours.

God will surely make it come to pass when you pray to Him. Our prayers go to God just like the process of rainfall. When the cloud is full of rain it empties on the earth.

No matter how long it takes to pray, no matter how things delay, it shall not kill your faith. If you are dealing with God, you must be patient to get your desire.

When you have a need, you will be able to relate with God to get it, and God is happy to see you come to Him because you believe He will give it to you. Also on the process of aspiring to that need you will encounter God.

If God has a time for you, you must wait. You can't determine for God His timing for your life. Wait on Him to supply all your needs.

When God command; this was not our idea, we never asked to be there or here or even to start a Ministry, it was God's idea, so it is his work, and we just obey. Elijah heard from God and was bold enough to work up to a King and tell him some hard words – there shall be neither dew nor rain these years, except by my word (1 Kings 17:1). Then following God's command, he went and waited at a brook. God provide food in a miraculous way for him! He commanded the ravens to sustain him with food. " The raven brought him bread and meat each morning and evening" (1 Kings 17:6).

After the water dried up, God sent Elijah to Zarephath. In that village, God perform another amazing act of provision. This time, the food did not come by way of birds, but by a simple request made by the prophet to a widow (1 King 17:13). She obeys and God did the rest.

The pattern here is very simple. It is our work to follow as God leads, and then obey the things he asks us to do. As we follow him, he will provide not what we necessary want but what we truly need. He will provide what we truly need even in amazing ways.

When God command just obey, it will protect, sustain and preserve your life, but when you disobey you will destroy yourself. When God command, it comes with blessings or judgment. The disobedient prophet in 1 Kings Chapter 13, because he have disobey the word of the Lord and have not keep the commandment which the Lord God commanded him, but have come back and eaten bread and drink water in the place of which the lord said to him, "You shall not eat bread nor drink water" ; when he had gone, a lion meet him by the road and killed him.

When God command is for our own good or preservation. His word or commands are the ways that God himself has chosen to preserve, sustain and bless us together and works all things for our good. His word or commandment is an immeasurable treasure, and in them we find God's matchless gift to his people.

Based on that we are move simply to trust in his providence as he leads us through our life.

Chapter Six

Some Helpful Hints

To succeed in ministry, you must labour in the word of God and in prayer, labour, in prayer and labour in Bible studies. This is what distinguishes us from ordinary people. Acts 6:4 says, "But we will give ourselves continually to prayer, and to the ministry of the word." When you labour in prayer and the word, God will do for you what He did not do for other people. This is the way to breakthrough in life and ministry. Those great men of God excelled because of their great sacrifices and labour in the word.

- Your breakthrough (success) in life depends on the level of your spiritual growth or maturity. When you attain a certain level of spirituality, you will produce a fruit to the world.

- The work of the ministry is not for one man and it is not a one man business. That is why God frustrates any attempt of one man to dominate the work of His ministry. Jesus, for example, did not heal all the people. Not all of the people that Jesus ministered to were healed but he left some of it for Peter or other disciples to do. Today also God lifts many people to do the work of ministry and God left others who are not healed for you to come and do it (heal them). (2 Timothy 4:2-6)

- The work of preaching the gospel is for all believers. Jesus commanded us to go and teach all nations, teaching them His word. (Matthew 28:18-20) We are to publish the good news of Christ. Ministry is not only for pastors but also for people having the grace and the gift of the spirit. Ministry also is a gift. Having them is a gift of ministry. Wait on your ministry to receive grace and also do initiative to promote the kingdom.

- To work on your spirit, you must dwell in God's presence. When you spend time in God's presence, all fear will go and you will be sure in your spirit that all will be well or in peace. For those who want to excel in school, as a student you can work on your spirit so that you can receive information on where your teacher is heading. A Christian is a person with a sharp conscious not a dead conscious.

- There are various ways through which God speaks to us. You have to discover how God speaks to you through the various ways He speaks or communicates to you.

- The Bible is general but how can you get the word of God for you? You must hear the voice of God; the voice of God is the right of every child of God. You need to hear His voice to know what God wants you to do per time.

- You can hear the voice of God by practically always finding time to be with God and meditating.

- When you hear the voice of God, you will be established. It helps you to have direction, enables you to live and delivers you from danger.

- You need the voice of God to stand against what man said you will not pass or excel.

- When you are in tune with His voice, He will tell you everything about a person and then you become secure or protected from future danger, e.g. in the issue of marriage. The voice of God gives you current information that you need at a time, the current or today's solution.

- When you seek God, you will receive divine enablement; the hand of God will rest in you and you will succeed in anything you are doing. (See Psalm 34:10) You can also seek God by being in the place where God is magnified or in the presence of His fellowship, e.g. fellowship of God's people.

- We must go to God every time, every moment by moment. There are different strategies as there are different situations, so every situation has its own peculiar or unique way of handling it so there is the need for moment by moment going to Him.

- In everything we do, we need to go to God for help and guidance. When you seek the face of God, God will arrange things for you that you will be surprised.

- How to seek divine guidance? Answer, ask: Read Matthew 7:7, 1 Kings 3:10.

- Forget the past, press toward the mark for the price. (Philippians 3:13-14)

- Be courageous! Don't allow people to discourage you; be bold as you are sure of your calling.

- Hope to keep moving: walk in His laws, (word) and remember His works and His wonders that He has shown you.

- It is the Holy Spirit that gives meaning or relevance to the work of God or what we do. Also is Him that gives power and boldness for witnessing.

- The Holy Spirit teaches all things; not only spiritual things but He also teaches secular things.

- When you are serving God, the devil is jealous of you, you need prayers. Always ask God to protect and preserve you. Peter escaped from prison because of prayers.

- Categories of the future: we have the immediate future, near future and far future and God knows how to handle the situation and to carry His children through. There is also eternal future, the eternity one, life after death. Jesus has summarized everything about our future. Read John 14:1-14. There are rooms, there are opportunities, and there are things to do.

- Have a dream. A dream is a driven force. Joseph had a dream. But you should be careful how you share your dream because there are dream killers or discouragers. Also, you need someone to introduce you to your dream or something that will announce you.

- From the days of John the Baptist until now, the kingdom of heaven has been taking it by force (Matthew 11:12).

- For you to advance forcefully there must be a discovery.

- When you are determined to do something good, God will be there to help you. John was consciously seeking God before he heard what God was saying. (Revelation 1:10)

- There is automatic faith when in the manifest presence of God; every doubt disappears.

- Make discoveries; it is in the process of seeking God that God will tell you something. God shows or reveals His ways to Moses but to the children of Israel, He acts.

- What controls the eternal is the spiritual. If there is going to be something it has already been concluded in the spirit. There must be success in the spirit before it will be successful in the physical. Life is in the hand of God.

- Develop character to sustain before God hands over things to us. God makes us to be patient, learn to wait on God's timing in order to develop character to sustain things.

- People react differently to the same situation. Good character enables you not to be driven or carried away by the condition or situation of an environment.

- Jesus live in the heart of people like you and I if you believe.

- Taking simple steps towards what God is calling you to will open new doors of opportunity.

Chapter Seven

The Lord Is Your Shepherd

The Lord is my shepherd; I shall not want.
(Psalm 23:1)

As a minister of God, you don't need to go around begging money from people. God is the one who sponsors His work. If God sends you, he will sponsor you and when God leads, He provides. If God calls you, He will be there to back the call. God will look or search for resources to sponsor His work on the earth.

God's resource is in His word and in His Spirit. God can work behind the scene and stir His people to give for His work through the prompting and stirring of the Spirit. It is the work of the Spirit of God to convince the people of God to give in support for God's work. God is more interested in our salvation than our finances. There is no limit to the way God uses to provide or finance His project or vision on the earth. And when God uses you to give or provide for His work, there is always a blessing in it.

Proverbs 11:24-25 tells us, "It is possible to give away and become richer! It is also possible to hold on too tightly and lose everything." Yes, the liberal man shall be rich! By watering others, he waters himself. (TLB)

God's word also says when we honour the Lord with our substance and all our increase our barns shall be filled with plenty.

It is lack of faith that make ministers or people of God to go around begging for things. God wants His children to trust Him for their needs or finances. I believe ministers can be stable, safe, and joyful because God promises to provide for His work here on the earth. There is power of hope, the power of faith – God's power is released when we pray in faith, work in faith, trusting and believing Him because faith pleases Him. Expectancy is an attribute of faith. Faith reaches out into the spiritual realm and expects God's supernatural power to show up and do what no person on earth could do. Doubt, on the other hand, is afraid nothing good will happen; it does not please God and is not something He tends to bless. We are powerless when we live with doubt, disappointment, and lack of confidence in God.

We know that faith in God is foundational to ministry work or to answered prayer so it stands to reason that doubt and unbelief – which are opposites of faith – will keep our prayers from being answered. Faith is a powerful spiritual dynamic and is something God responds to and without opposition. Satan will attack our minds with doubt, unbelief, and questioning and when he does, we need to check in with our hearts and see what they say. We can believe something in our hearts even when our minds question it and we need to go with what is in our hearts and not with what is in our heads. We are not supposed to believe our doubts; we are supposed to doubt our doubts and believe our God.

One of the keys to overcome doubts and unbelief is found in Hebrews 12:2 which says, "Looking away (From all that will distract) to Jesus, who is the leader and the source of our faith… and is also its finisher…" Many times, doubts and unbelief start with distraction. When we are distracted from God's promises or God's ability to come through for us, then we begin to doubt. We start thinking more and more about our problems or our challenges to diminish. But we need to do what Hebrews 12:2 says to do and keep looking to Jesus. In order to resist doubt and stay in faith, we need to stare at Him, at His goodness, at His ability to help us, at His love for us.

Keeping our eyes off everything that would steal our faith or distract us from what God says is the antidote to doubt and unbelief. We have to remember that he is the source of our faith and He finishes what He starts – so there is no reason to doubt.

The apostle James said that when we doubt, we become double–minded and the double- minded man receives nothing he asks from God because he is unstable in all of his ways. (See James 1:6-8) We need to decide what we believe and not change our minds when our circumstances begin to waver. We need to remember that John 11:40 promises that we will see the glory of God if we will only believe!

Chapter Eight

Avoid The Quest For Materialism

This world is not our home – we are just passing through. So often ministers fall into the confines of this world's values and strive toward earthly goals. We endeavour to reach the peak of our vision; we budget our money and invest a chunk of every pay into various valuable possessions to feel the status of success. We believe that these accomplishments are the things that fulfil our purpose in life and so they are worth the struggle and the endurance. But this thinking is wrong.

This world is not our home; we are just passing through. The pressures to meet the material goals of this world have caused many ministers to believe that they need to struggle to achieve them in order to be successful but this is not a prerequisites set out by God. He tells us to keep our eyes on heaven and to not make earth our treasure.

"Don't store up treasures here on earth where they can erode away or may be stolen." (Matthew 6:19 TLB)

Our accomplishments are nothing that we have earned or collected here on earth and our purpose in life should not be focused on getting them. Our eyes, our hearts and our values should all be on Jesus and what He has done for us and our goal and our focus should be on Him and on our home in eternity with Him. The rewards that we look forward to are not only earthly. We take the concept of faith and abuse it as a tool to try to employ God to make us wealthy.

Doesn't God want us to be happy? Does He want us to live in poverty? Not at all. God wants us to have a fulfilling life on earth and He does not want us to be poor. He says in 3 John 2 that it is His will for us to prosper and be in health.

When our heart lives for Him, He provides these things for us. We don't need to scheme to get them or to make them our quest as a Christian. Our quest should be on things or places that will live through eternity with Him.

This world, on the other hand, is coming to its end and has become a target for distraction. We don't need to look far to see that it is falling apart; that crime, poverty and natural disasters are growing astronomically and that diseases and starvation have become epidemic nightmares around the globe. Jesus tells us that we are living in the last days on earth's existence. "But know this, that in the last days perilous times will come…" (2 Timothy 3:1)

The earth is not going to get better; it will continue downhill until God destroys it. "Heaven and earth will pass away, but my words will by no means pass away…" (Matthew 24:5)

While we are still here, though, we have a purpose to fulfil as Christians and that is to encourage and support each other and to be witness to the word of God's grace through Jesus Christ our savior. Our lives should reflect God so when people see us they see the character and the spirit of God in us.

How do we do that? By the way we act and react to situations; by the way we give God all the praises and glory for being our Lord and our help when we need help (Psalm 9:9) and by the way we live our lives and show that Jesus is our reason for living and that our wealth is not in earthly possessions but in the eternal life He has prepared for us.

We cannot put our hope and our purpose in earthly riches. We cannot take them with us as they belong to this world. If we cling to the possessions of this world, we will die just like Lot's wife died when God led his family out of Gomorrah. She looked in sadness because her heart was in that city and its possessions and not with the Lord.

We can enjoy the good things that this world has to offer but we cannot be attached to them; they cannot be our goals for this life. Why? Because when we are attached and when we live to collect these possessions, they become gods to us and what does the Bible says about that? "You shall have no other gods before me…" (Deuteronomy 5:7) It is a very fine line that separates the natural instincts of setting up a nice home for our family and wanting only the best and most expensive possessions for our personal comfort and social status. God says in Isaiah 32:18, "My people will dwell in dwellings, and in quiet resting places." He wants us to have a good home to live in here and He wants us to be healthy and He even wants to give us the desires of our hearts. All these things are ours because He loves us and we love Him. We are not part of this world anymore and we don't depend upon this world to survive, we depend on God for everything. When we make heaven our goal and our home to look forward to, the things we have are simply needs or desires to get us through this journey. Yes, they may be nice things, but they are not our reason to want to stay here. We are not attached to them.

Our hearts are free to enjoy them or to give then away. We share what we have with other Christians so that we all are part of God's blessing and we help those in need which in turn shows Jesus to a hurting world. And when we do, we are blessed.

We should not spend our time, money or thoughts on making this world our permanent home but while we are here God promises to supply all our needs. He says in Matthew 6:33, "But seek first the kingdom of God and His righteousness, and all these things shall be added to you."

This world is not our home. It is a battlefield where the devil is trying to steal, kill and destroy anyone and everyone so he can keep them from knowing God. Our commission as Christians and ministers is to arm ourselves in the word and through the power of the Holy Spirit; we can share the gospel with people and win souls for Christ. And we can do this because heaven is our home; heaven is our goal, and heaven is where we want to be.

The Laws Of Giving And Receiving

In Luke 6:38, Jesus said, "Give and it will be given to you..."

Here Jesus is trying to reveal to us the law governing the universe. In science, we study the law found in the creation. Men have studied the universe in which we live. They have found that there are laws governing it; e.g. there are laws of physics and chemistry. These laws were not originated by men but only discovered. These laws existed before men discovered them. It has taken more intelligence, knowledge and hard work just to discover these laws. Men did not make these laws. Did nature make these Laws? No, nature has no mind; nature is dumb, blind and deaf. No, nature could not have made the laws that govern nature. Did these laws come about by chance; chance is random, disorderly, and destructive. Chance also is dumb, blind and deaf. No, chance could not have originated the laws of creation.

Scientists have found that the laws of the universe are mathematical in nature. These mathematical laws were not invented by men but only found to exist already.

Mathematics shows rationality in the order of the universe. In physics and engineering mechanics, experience has proven the mathematical law to be a reality. For example, men were sent to the moon and they were even brought back. The calculation was accurate. The rationality of mathematical law in the universe demands the seasonal intelligent origin.

To accept science, one must logically believe in God who created science.

Yes, the laws of the universe demand an intelligent law giver. The laws of physic show the great physicist. The laws of chemistry show the great chemist. In the Bible, the great law giver calls himself God. He is the creator of the havens and earth.

It is he who made earth by his power, who established the world by his wisdom, and by his understanding he has stretched out the heavens. (Jeremiah 10:12)

The laws governing the universe reveal that if you want to receive you must give. A law which Jesus himself confirms it, "Give and it shall be given to you: good measure, pressed down, shaken together, and running over will be put into your bosom."

For with the same measure that you use it will be measured back to you."(Luke 6-38)

If you give little, you will receive little, if you give much you will receive much. Giving is an opportunity for investment. Our giving must first be to God and to humanity. Also giving is not only restricted to money, but in any aspect of our life. We must first give ourselves to God for his work and for his service or purpose on the earth. If you give or sow money, you will reap, get or harvest money. If you give love you will reap, get or harvest love. If you give or sow charity, you will reap, get or harvest charity. The seed sown determines the harvest you will receive.

There is always a reward for everything that we do here on the earth. Proverb 11:25 tells us, "The liberal's soul shall be made fat: and he that watereth shall be watereth also himself."

Proverbs 3:9, 10 tells or promise us when you honour the lord with your substance, and with all the first fruit of all your increase so shall your business, account filled with plenty.

God Almighty not only promises to prosper those who give but he promises to preserve that which he prospers you with.

Proverbs 11:24 says, "There is he that scattereth, and yet increaseth…"

John Bunyan used to say: "There was a man in our town; some folks did think him mad; the more he gave away, the more he had."

The law of sowing and reaping applies to the whole realm of generosity. "For if you give, you will get! Your gifts will return to you in fill and over flowing measure, pressed down, shaken together to make room for more, and running over. Whatever measure you use to give-large or small will be used to measure what is given back to you." (Luke 6:38 TLB)

He who sows sparingly will also reap sparingly, and he who sows bountifully will also reap bountifully. A word from Jesus for it.

Now this is not mechanical or automatic. It works by the creative power of God the great giver.

People are to sow as God sows love and goodness; with joyful free will. "Each one must do as he has made up his mind," said Paul, "not reluctantly or under compulsion."

God loves a cheerful giver.

Then he spoke again of the reward. This is always dangerous in a way. For people by nature want to control things or dictate to God the timing and terms of result. What Paul said is that God is able to provide you with every blessing in abundance so that you may always have enough for everything. (2 Corinthians 9:8) But beware God gives this by his grace not on our demand.

Furthermore, "enough of everything "is by God's measure of what is enough for us not the measure of our ever-growing greed and rising wants.

Paul believed that if Christians are generous in contributing to the Lord's work, there will be reward spilling over and returning to the giver sufficient for his needs and enough for him to go on providing "in abundance in every good work".

ChapTer Ten

Yardstick For Measuring Success In Ministry

The ways of the world and God's way of success are not the same. Success in God's eyes is those who do with excellence the thing he called them to do. He measured our success by how well we do what he called us to do. It relents to the assignment not in the abundance of materialism. It is not what you get or have that makes you successful, it is who you are. When you are following his game plan for life, you cannot fail. Even if we don't have the money, God is with us and with God we can achieve more or do more in life.

Success is being where God puts you and doing faithfully what he called you to do.

We are glad we have God that can do exceedingly more than we have. All we need in life is to make God the centre of our life. He will keep in perfect peace all those who trust in him, whose thoughts turn often to him. (Isaiah 26:3)

A happy life is one filled not only with sunshine but one which uses both light and shadow to produce beauty.

This indicates that whatever was required of Jesus in his coming to the earth is also required of believers. Whatever manner, whatever purpose, whatever sacrifice, whatever motivation that characteristised Christ on his mission in the world must also characterize his servant in the world. As it was with our saviour, so it must be with his servants in the world.

"Looking unto Jesus the author and finisher of our faith; who for the joy that was set before him endured the cross, despising the shame, and is set down at the right hand of the throne of God." (Hebrews 12:2 KJV)

Jesus teaches the whole counsel of God which involves a full or bed presentation of truth.

Balance is the key to life. Any truth taken to the extreme that ignores other aspects is unbalanced and can be harmful.

Hyper-prosperity preachers primarily emphasize scriptures that deal with personal blessing and financial prosperity. Although there is some truth in their teachings, this overemphasis produces believers who seek the blessing more than the blessed. It can also produce false expectation of people who sow their money into a ministry expecting a hundred returns which rarely, if ever, happens on a purely financial level.

I believe in Biblical prosperity but not in a "right centered" gospel that ignores our Biblical stewardship to produce wealth primarily to confirm his covenant in the earth. (Deuteronomy 8:18)

The hyper-dispensation believes they have to passively wait for the rapture and avoid political and social reform because trying to transform culture is like "re-arranging the chairs on the Titanic". I do believe there will be some sort of strong kingdom influence in the nations; read Matthew 25:32, before the second coming, all of the major Biblical covenants and themes point to a victorious church and victorious gospel before the end of human history, read the following verse.

Genesis 1:28 says, "...and God blessed them, and God said unto them, be fruitful and multiply and replenish the earth and subdue it and have dominion over the fish of the sea, and over the fowl of the air; and over every living thing moveth upon the earth." (KJV)

Genesis 12:1-3 says, "Now the Lord had said unto Abraham, get thee out of thy country, and from thy kindred, and from thy fathers house, unto a land that I will show thee; and I will make of thee a great nation, and I will bless thee, and make thy name great; and thou shalt be a blessing; and I will bless them that bless thee, and curse him that curseth thee; and in thee shall all the families of the earth be blessed."

Genesis 22:17-18 says, "That in blessing I will bless thee and in multiplying I will multiply thy seed as the stars of the heaven, and as the sand which is upon the sea shore; and thy seed shall possess the gate of his enemies; and in thy seed shall all the nations of the earth be blessed; because thou hast obeyed my voice."

Psalm 110:2 says, "The Lord shall send the rod of thy strength out of Zion; rule thou in the midst of thine enemies."

Acts 3:21 says, "Whom the heaven must receive until the times of restitution of all things which God hath spoken by the mouth of all his holy prophets since the world began."

The hyper-rational; those in this camp are afraid of any spiritual experiences or manifestations. They depend upon their mind to the neglect of their spirit. They believe God only speaks through his written word. They rationalize their life and have little or substantive fellowship with God. They split hairs over Biblical doctrines and in some ways worship the Bible more than the God of the Bible. Jesus said it is possible to study the scriptures without coming to God. In John 5:39-40 Jesus says, "Search the scriptures; for in them ye think ye have eternal life; and they are they which testify of me. And ye will not come to me, that ye might have life." Another translation of Jesus' words reads, "You search the scriptures, for you believe they give you eternal life. And the scriptures point to me! Yet you won't come to me so that I can give you this life eternal!" (TLB)

In conclusion, whenever we focus on a truth to the exclusion of other aspects of truth we end up in error.

May God help us to understand and preach the whole counsel of God so that we can feed the flock of God and equip them to fulfil their divine purpose.

Chapter Eleven

Ministry Work And Working For A Living

Success in ministry work does not depend on having a large or big ministry and it does not depend on having material things. Success depends on being the man God wants you to be, living and doing your God-given purpose and being or doing what he created you to be or become.

Success in ministry depends on God's divine guidance for your life and this involves moment by moment guidance by the spirit of God.

When a minister lives in God's providential guidance for his life there, will be open doors; a door to minister and a door for divine provision. Living in God's providential guidance for your life, there is always a divine provision. God will always have a way or open door to take care of his creature. Jesus said, "Behold the fowls of the air: for they sow not, neither do they reap, nor gather into barns: yet your heavenly father feedeth them. Are ye not much better than they?" (Matthew 6:26)

Ministers should learn to have faith in God that He will take care of them. God can take care of you even if you don't have a big ministry to support or sustain you. God has a way to meet our every need even without the support of the people we do minister to. He has all the power to take care of every minister even if they are without visible means of support. (See Matthew 17:27)

Even if your ministry is to minister to a small group, or to do a little or a small thing or responsibility in the kingdom of God, do it with all your heart and with all your might. As long as you are faithful to your calling, being in the place he wants you to be, he will take care of you.

Also, you should not be discouraged on the one hand simply because your particular ministry is not as outstanding as that of another, but at the same time, you should never rest till you know what God's plan is for your life and until in the power of His spirit you are doing his will.

Righteous or Godly Source or Provision in the Work of the Ministry

Godly means to act like God, to have a perspective of God, to think and do things God's way or to think and do things like him, to relate with people the way God relates with them.

God does not want gimmicks, or trying to force somebody to give through compulsion, as if our ministry depends on people. God should be our source, supply and sustainer, and where he leads or direct us, on what to do, he will provide.

Some men are clever and experts in forcing people to give to them and they employ all kind of human wisdom or knowledge to convince people to contribute for the good or nice work they do. But this is completely unacceptable to God; if we do that we are making human beings our source and not dependent on God. It also reveals our lack of faith in God to supply all our needs according to his riches in glory by Christ Jesus.

I am not against people begging for money or asking for financial help to do work but we should not endeavour to force people to give for our work. We should not disrespect, mistreat, use or take people for granted. You have to be strong to earn respect. Stop using people!

If you think God is leading you that way just say it once and leave the rest to God. Let God be the one to convince his people. Let your yes be yes and your no be no.

Men who specialize in employing all means to lure or force people to finance their project did not understand God opens doors or his riches in glory to supply all our needs. God will open new doors of opportunity when we take simple steps towards what he called to us to do.

God hates begging and he wants everybody to work and trust him for financial provision.

My advice to us who are ministers is that if we have something, people will follow us or come to us when we attempt to complete godly agendas, Apart from doing them God's way and being in his will, we are merely boxing the air.

Working for a Living

Paul employs this kind of method to support his own ministry. Paul supported his own ministry with a trade (tent making) rather than taking funds from others. He did this to avoid suspicions that he was profiting financially from his spiritual work. In 1 Thessalonians 2:9 he says, "For ye remember, brethren, our labour and travail: for labouring night and day, because we would not be chargeable unto any of you, we preached unto you the gospel of God."

As we were allowed of God to be put in trust with the gospel, let us speak not as pleasing men, but God, which tried our hearts. Also, we should not at any time use flattering words, nor a cloke of covetousness. With the Thessalonians, his hard work gave another advantage: it set a good example for those who were quitting their jobs.

When Paul lived with the Thessalonians, he was gentle and loving, like a mother cares for her little children, like a nurse cherishes her children. (1 Thessalonians 2:7)

Absent from them, he wrote if he had only them on his mind all day, in 1 Thessalonians, he praised their strength, fussed over report of their weaknesses and continually prayed and thanked God for their spiritual progress.

He also exhorted and comforted and charged every one of them, as a father doth his children. We should be so affectionately desirous of people or believers we minister to, we should be willing to have imparted unto them not the gospel of God only, but also our own souls, because they are dear unto us, that they would walk worthy of God who hath called them unto his kingdom and glory.

Chapter Twelve

The Secret Of Successful And Thriving
Ministries Or Godly Services

The book of Revelation unveils Jesus' letters to the leaders of the church. This being letters to the seven churches in Asia Minor (Revelation 1-3) letter to the seven churches in Turkey, to the church in Ephesus, the one in Smyrna, and those in Pergamos, Thyatira Sardis, Philadelphia and Laodicea.

To the church in Laodicea, I know thy works, that thou art neither could nor hot: I would thou wert cold or hot. So then because thou art lukewarm, and neither cold nor hot, I will spew thee out of my mouth: Because thou sayest, I am rich, and increased with goods, and have need of nothing; and knowest not that thou art wretched, and miserable, and poor, and blind, and naked." (Rev. 3-15-17)

These are the words of the Lord Jesus. The message is given by Christ to the church of Laodicea, the last mention of the seven churches in Asia Minor to whom the spirit sent messages by John, the writer of Revelation. The message seems especially given for the last days. The message to Laodicea just precedes the story of coming of Christ for his saints as pictured in Revelation 4:1. "I know thy works," Jesus said. He knows the human heart and that which seems all well to the casual observer is nauseating to God.

"I know that you think you are well off," says Jesus. "You say, 'I am rich, and increased with goods, and have need of nothing, and knowest not that thou art poor and wretched and miserable and blind and naked.'"

Who are those that make God vomit? Who are these that must spew out of his mouth with disgust? Not the infidel! Not the atheist! Not the unregenerate sinner! He does not mean the man who denies his atonement for sinners. He does not mean those who are out-and-out for the devil, those who are unconverted. They have never been in intimate touch with Christ; how can he spew them out? They have never known his conscious and happy presence; then how can they lose it? They have never have the sweet communion that a child of God may have, not the power of the Holy Spirit, or soul-winning influence; how then can Christ spew them out? One who is not a branch of Christ can never wither as Christ's branches sometimes do. (John 15:6) Unless one has preached the gospel, he could not become a castaway that is, laid on the shelf with his ministry ruined as Paul feared he might be. (1 Cor. 9:27)

It is because they are lukewarm that they nauseate the saviour. It is because they are not hot for the ministry of God. The people in the churches and ministries, not those on the outside, nauseate God. To lukewarm Christians God says, "I will spew thee out of my mouth."

The Secret of Successful and Thriving Ministry is to be Hot, Red Hot in our Work for God

Jesus prefers us to be desperate with the Bible, obedience or obeying the Holy Spirit, agreeable to believe. Christ desires that all his own be on fire for God, filled with Spirit, endued with a Holy favour for God. But if you are not red or hot, then Jesus will not keep your ministry or service prospering or thriving.

John R. Rice writes, "Of course you feel that it is better to be a lukewarm Christian than to be a lost sinner going to hell. And for you it is better. You had rather go to heaven though by your indifferent living, your lukewarm heart, and your pallid Christianity you send a thousand others to hell!" And that is what many Christians really do. If you have fully trusted in Christ and so have been born again, you will go to heaven. But if you are a lukewarm Christian, you thwart the gospel and damn other souls. All some people will ever know of Christ is what they see in you. And what they see in you, many do not want. They see no victory over sin, no Christian joy, no sincere testimony. They see no evidence of a changed heart, no proof of the reality of Christ and salvation to the believer. The gospel as you live it contradicts the gospel preachers preach. Lukewarm Christians are the alibi of sinners, the decoy ducks of Satan. <u>Lukewarm Christians are double crossers of Christ, spiritual adulteress who do more harm than good.</u>"[2]

A fervent, godly missionary in a field can often win more souls than an equally earnest preacher with assistance of a church of a thousand members. A lukewarm church may insulate a whole community against the gospel, or an indifferent family can make it impossible to win unsaved loved ones. So, for the sake of others, Christ says, "I will come unto thee quickly, and will remove thy candle

---

[2] John R. Rice, church members who make God sick, P.5.

stick out of his place, except thou repent." (Rev. 2:5 b) He would rather you would be cold if not hot, that you will be out – and – out for the devil if you are not-and-out for God. You will do less harm as an infidel than as a lukewarm church member. The damning blight of today is too many Christians - that is, too many of the kind that we have, too many indifferent and lukewarm, nominal Christians. If there were only one-tenth as many people who made any pretence of faith in Christ, and if every one of these were spiritually on fire, filled with spirit of God, joyful, victorious, loving witnessing, sacrificing Christians, then what a revival there would be!

How well pleased we are with ourselves! Our complacency is, in fact, the very heart of our sin! If we were burdened about our own faults, if we could see our own shallowness, our own insincerity, our own spiritual poverty, our own blindness, then God would not be nauseated and disgusted with us. But Jesus said to the lukewarm Christians of Laodicea that he will spew them out "because thou sayest I am rich and increased with goods and have need of nothing, and knowest not that thou art wretched, and miserable, and poor, and blind, and naked." That is the reason he must vomit us out of his mouth or cause our ministry to closed, not shining and not prospering or thriving.

Oh, the sin of our self-satisfaction! We have beautiful church houses; we have more modern church equipment than ever before. We have splendid organizations. We have preachers with doctor's degrees. We have large budgets. We have literature and radio programs. We have denominational schools and hospitals. The most influential people in town are members of our churches. We are rich and we have need of nothing! So we think, but to God, our smirking self-righteousness, our being so well pleased with ourselves, is an abomination. We do not know that we are wretched and miserable and poor and blind and naked! Our lukewarmness is simply a phase of our unbelief, of our unconfessed sin, of our love for the world. It proves our estrangement from God, our disregard of the Holy Spirit's leading. We are so full of self and the world that we have no hunger for God. We do not have, and God help us we do not want!

In the Binghamton Theatre in Binghamton, New York, 1936, in a revival service sponsored by a number of churches, John R. Rice preached, "Sodom, Gomorrah and Binghamton; three of a kind." A group of learnt preachers, meeting in the city, took heated exception to his sermon subject. A prominent denominational official said that for Binghamton, with it schools and hospitals, art and industry, its progressive and intelligent people, to be compared with ancient Sodom was unthinkable! His remarks were printed in the daily press. However, the night in a big club, within a block of the theatre where he preached, was held a very big saturnalia of debauch and sin. Fifty prostitutes were brought in from New York City. The most prominent men in the city bought tickets to the banquet and show. By midnight, many of the men were drunk and many of the women were naked and by 4 o'clock in the morning, he was told officers had to stop the breaking of furniture and had to interfere with the wild carousal. Literally, hundreds took part. Many were members of the churches where these pious and complacent preachers held forth. Investigations revealed that such orgies were frequent affairs. Many of the preachers were openly modernistic, denying the deity of Christ, the blood atonement, the new birth, and the inspiration of the Bible, and they were shocked at the comparison of Binghamton to Sodom and Gomorrah. They were rich, increased with goods and had need of nothing, they thought. But God knew that they were "wretched and miserable and poor, and blind, and naked".[2]

I announce this same sermon subject to our world today. In newspapers, we read shocking revelations about the wickedness going on in our

<u>cities while most of the preachers either did not know or did not care.</u> [3]

I say we are a self-satisfied lot. We are lukewarm Christians. And may God forgive us for that self-satisfaction is the thing that makes us hopeless of the blessing of God. We feel we have need of nothing so we seek nothing and find nothing! We are not hungry; so we will not eat! We are not thirsty; so we will not drink! We are not conscious of lack of power; so we do not seek power. We do not realize how our sins grieve God; so we do not confess them nor forsake them. We do not feel any special need to pray; so we do not pray. We do not weep, we do not fast, and we do not confess our sins! May God awake us self-satisfied Christians before we are spewed out of the mouth of God, before we are permanently lay aside never to be used in his service any more.

Signs of a Dying Church or Ministry

The word of God teaches us that there are times God's presence can leave the corporate expression of his people; we see this in 1 Samuel 4:21-22 when the name Ichabod was given to the grandson of Eli, the priest after the ark of the covenant was

---

[3] John R. Rice, church members who make God sick P.8.

captured by the Philistines. Also, in book of Revelation 3:1 Jesus told the church of the Sardis that they have a reputation of being alive but was dead. It is possible for communities of faith to be dead or dying. In Revelation 2:5, Jesus warned the church of Ephesus that if they do not repent, he would remove their lampstand. The lampstand represents the true church or ministry according to Revelation 1:20. Jesus wanted to shut down the churches or remove himself from it because the church was dead spiritually. It is impossible for Satan to close down a church because Jesus said that the gates of hell will not prevail against the church (Matthew 16). Whenever a church or ministry ceases to exist, it is the Lord Himself who shut it down. This is the reason many congregations and ministries close their doors every year.

Some Signs of a Dead Church or Dying Ministry

1. There are no functional prayer gatherings. Within dying churches, few people show up to pray and seek God since they have no sense of his presence or that he is present in the mist of them. If you think God is communicating (e.g. communion of the Holy Spirit) you will be motivated to speak to him and listen to him.

2. There are no expectations for answered prayers. Few, if any, pray to him since there is no anticipation that God will actually answer prayer. When you are in a church without faith to believe God, it is either dead or dying.

3. The presence of God is missing in the assembly of the saints. The heavens are closed over dead or dying churches or ministries. There is no sense of God's presence during worship.

4. The power of God is not manifest. Jesus said that when demons were cast out it was a sign the kingdom of God was among them. (Luke 11:20) It was expected that the miraculous to be the norm in the life of the church or ministries. (Galatians 3:5) Jesus expected believers to use their faith to receive answer to prayers and move mountains. (Mark 11:23-24) When there are no instances of God's divine intervention in a church or ministry, it can be a sign that the church or ministry is dead or dying.

5. The word of God is presented without authority. The religious leaders who practice a dead faith during Jesus' time where shocked when they had Jesus speak because he taught

with authority. (Mark 1:22) In dead or dying churches, the preacher has no unction to instil faith, motivate action or convict of sin.

6. No regular addition of saved people. In the early churches, the Lord regularly added people to the church to be saved. Acts 2:27 says, "Praising God and having favour with all the people. And the Lord added to the church daily such as should be saved."

7. No room for the Holy Spirit of God to operate when every aspect of the message and the preaching is predictable as if choreographed to the minute, it may reveal there is no room for the Holy Spirit to operate. Like Samson of old, the spirit may have departed without the people knowing it. (Judges 16:20) Any aspect of our church or ministry that functions without dependence on the Holy Spirit shows that it is a machination of men and not of God.

8. There is no disciple making. The bottom line in all churches is the making of committed Christ followers. It does not matter how large a church is, what matters is how many matured sons are being developed that will positively affect the created order. (Romans 8:19-21)

9. The people jockey for positions and titles. When people are not seeking the glory of God, they depend more upon getting affirmation from men. A church or ministry without the presence of God will have hierarchical culture with people posturing for positions and titles. The less you know God intimately, the more your identity will be connected to credentials and titles.

10. There is no sense of divine mission and purpose. When there is no vision, the people perish. (Proverbs 29:18) When a church or ministry is dead or dying, they have no compelling transcendent purpose that motivates them to fulfil their Biblical calling.

11. Few people volunteer to serve. In a dead or dying church or ministry, there will be no willingness to serve; very few people volunteer to serve in the ministry. Psalms 110:3 says that people shall be willing in the day of his power, that is, the people will volunteer or offer themselves willingly in the day of his power.

12. Few people support the church or the ministry with tithes and offerings. Jesus said, "Where your treasure is, there your heart will be." (Matthew 6:21) When a church or

ministry is dying or dead, few people will be motivated to invest their finances into it. Conversely, when people see God moving within the church or ministry, they will have more faith and be more motivated to give of their finances knowing that is being sown on good soil.

13. The community does not get imparted. Community development is part of the things in the kingdom of God. He wants to see our community developed and transform through our good works. God called believers to be salt of the earth and light of the world. (Matthew 5:13-16) When our lamps go out, the surrounding community is no longer changed by the power of the gospel. Furthermore, any so-called church or ministry revival that does not bring positive change to their surrounding community is not real revival.

In conclusion, if we see any of these signs in our churches or ministries, we shall ask the Lord to help and resuscitate it; ask him what he wants you to do. At times, in American history, the turn of 19th century, the church in general was in a very low spiritual state; God rose up men like Charles Finney to usher in the second great awakening which revived thousands of congregations and awaken lost sinners.

Like the prophet Habakkuk of old, let us seek the Lord to revive his work in the mist of the years and beseech him that in wrath he would remember mercy. (Habakkuk 3:2)

Truth Distribution

P. O. Box 712

Mubi, Adamawa State

Nigeria.

Tel: +2348067084428

Tel: +2348050672156

E-mail: truthdistribution521@gmail.com

Truth Distribution exists to edify, encourage and give hope to believers with the word of God through gospel publications and also to give faith to people, because faith comes through hearing or reading the word of God.

The knowledge of the word gives faith; it gives faith to the reader. Knowledge is so powerful that what you know could help you live a successful life.